*For Marjor[ie?]
with best wishes*

# Head and Shin

*Tim Thorne*

Walleah Press

Published by
Walleah Press
PO Box 368
North Hobart Tasmania 7002
Australia

Copyright © 2004 Tim Thorne

ISBN 1 877010 03 0

All rights reserved. No part of this publication may be reproduced, stored in a retrieval system, or transmitted in any form or by any means (electronic, mechanical, photocopying, recording, or otherwise), without the prior permission of both the copyright holder and the publisher.

Tasmania
ARTS TASMANIA

This project was assisted through Arts Tasmania by the Premier, Minister for the Arts.

Cover art, design and desktop production:
Cate Lowry, Fine Print, Hobart

to the memory of my two mothers,
Nita Thorne nee Pearce and
Betty Kent Wallace nee Hughes

# Acknowledgments

The poems in this collection include some which have previously appeared in the following publications:

*Critical Survey* (UK), *Famous Reporter, Four W, Heat, Island, Jacket, Meanjin, Moorilla Mosaic, Overland, Press Press, Republic Readings 6, Salt, Southerly, The Write Stuff, Ulitarra* and *Who is it?*

Some have been read over *ABC Radio National* and *City Park Radio*.

The section "The Streets Aren't for Dreamers" constitutes the greater part of a series of poems which was published as a separate chapbook by Shoestring Press (Nottingham 1995) and is reprinted here with kind permission.

# Contents

| | |
|---|---|
| Leipzig | 1 |
| To Adrian Paunescu | 2 |
| Crash | 5 |
| When the Saints Go Marching Out | 6 |
| Love Poem for Stephanie | 7 |
| Poem for Port Arthur | 8 |
| The Holy Tomato of Huddersfield | 9 |
| Chronicles of the King | 10 |
| Aerodynamics | 15 |
| Speaking for Myself | 16 |
| The Living are Left with Imagined Lives | 17 |
| Suter Hartmann & Rahtjen's Composition Co. Ltd | 18 |
| … and a Pound of Round | 19 |
| The Aisles | 20 |
| Love Poem (Dental) | 22 |
| Tens | 23 |
| Cold War | 24 |
| Coming Apart at the Scene | 25 |
| Brontë Country | 26 |
| Animal, Medical or Visceral | 27 |
| The Training of the Urban Guerrilla | 28 |
| Don Gibson and Etymology | 30 |
| Relaxed and Comfortable | 31 |
| Massive Quartzes | 32 |
| Erechtheus 33's Apologia | 34 |
| Knowing Your Place | 35 |
| Weeding my Grandparents' Grave | 36 |
| These Days You Need All the Work You Can Get | 37 |
| At Table | 38 |
| Keeping the Dream Alive | 39 |
| Et in Acadia Ego? | 40 |

| | |
|---|---:|
| "… good grammar / and an unclouded eye…" | 42 |
| Mother and Son | 43 |
| For my Father | 44 |
| Meditation on Parliament House, Canberra, 2002 | 46 |
| Dry | 47 |
| Zig-Zag Track | 48 |
| Scapeland | 49 |
| Writing the World | 50 |

## aUStralia

| | |
|---|---:|
| Oosutoraria | 53 |
| Vinegar Hill | 55 |
| Pinchgut | 56 |
| Jonathan Burke McHugo Comes to Town | 57 |
| Phrenology | 58 |
| Spider Dance and Horse Whip | 59 |
| Bangar | 60 |
| Mandarin of the Crystal Button | 61 |
| Coningham v Coningham | 62 |
| Black Cat and Wooden Shoe | 63 |
| Waldheim | 64 |
| The *Emden* | 65 |
| Diggers | 67 |
| Lockout | 68 |
| Many Happy Returns 26/1/1938 | 69 |
| The Mayor | 70 |
| Tanah Merah | 71 |
| Red Nest in Vital Mine | 72 |
| Lake Eyre Curse | 74 |
| Advent 21/12/1967 | 75 |
| Sight Screen | 76 |
| Footscray FC | 77 |

## The Streets Aren't For Dreamers

| | |
|---|---:|
| The Cull | 81 |
| Rat's Song | 82 |
| Stage Dive | 83 |
| Roadkill | 84 |
| Advice | 85 |
| Words for K | 86 |
| The Ballad of Tamieka Sharp, aged 15 | 87 |
| Saturday Night | 88 |
| Bouncer | 89 |
| Escort | 90 |
| Busking | 91 |
| The Hoon's Soliloquy | 92 |
| Arriving in Devonport | 93 |
| Blue Cow at the Trades | 94 |
| The Leaving | 95 |
| Bear | 96 |

## Chrome, Bone & Microphone

| | |
|---|---:|
| Life | 99 |
| Life Education for Rural Youth | 100 |
| Time | 102 |
| Road | 103 |
| Katoomba Tourist Poem | 104 |
| Encounter: A True Story | 105 |
| Lime-green Widgie | 106 |
| Too Old to Rap | 108 |
| The Ballad of Dennis Archer | 110 |
| All I've Planned and All I've Schemed | 111 |
| Aubade | 112 |
| The Nature of Australia | 113 |
| To Edmond's (*pace* Bill) | 114 |
| Ten Minute Man? | 115 |

| | |
|---|---|
| Midland Highway Blues | 116 |
| Pension Payday | 118 |
| Why my Heart Belongs to Rover | 119 |
| At the Book Launch | 120 |
| Ode to the Irenicists c. 1987 | 121 |
| Writing with Viagra | 122 |
| Galilee Revisited | 123 |
| Green and Blue: a love poem | 124 |
| My Mate Robbo | 125 |
| Salamanca Two Dog Blues | 126 |
| Rimbaud: First Blood | 127 |
| Everything, 2002 | 128 |
| Haiku | 129 |
| Cutting a Pretentious Tasmanian Poet Down to Size | 130 |

# Head and Shin

# Leipzig

Against Honecker's hoons
the *Gewandhaus* was sanctuary.
Masur stopped the show,
was a safe conductor.
Music, after all, formed
with Party and Sport
the Trinity.

Now *Deutschland über Alles*
in the square drowns out Bach
and Irving's apologia for Adolf
proves freedom of speech.
Where is the sanctuary
for those who shot through
the wall to the dole queues?

A 14-year-old girl with
shoulders as big as all of Prussia
does lonely laps in water
clean of chemicals and blood
against the clock,
against the clock.

# To Adrian Paunescu

This summer of lies
from Murdoch and CBS
was your winter of truth.

They trashed your villa,
pissed in your spa,
raped all your mistresses
with Coke bottles.
They will burn your books.

Another laureate
of the gilded left
was exiled there:
verse, luxury
*velut crimen* abhorred.

Metamorphoses:
subdued vox populi
to stag's troat;
"people's poet"
now, like Imelda's shoes
or Tammy's tears
a filler joke.

Empires today,
more scissile, less
able to withstand
the modish wowsers,
are easily replaced.
When the barbarians
come from the West
live via satellite
to what were satellites,
now centrifugally

at large, lassoable,
yet another (just what
the cowboy ordered)
Augustan age will spread
its bland and regular smog
over the provinces.

Raise your hand
and say after me:
"I want to buy.
I want the freedom
of brand names.
I want a Porsche
and a human right
and a ball-point pen
that really works.
Democracy's
the real thing."
Sign here.

Every age of course
should have its Alcaeus.
Eternal opposition
inspires, excites,
is good for an awkward laugh.
But it's a queer enough trade
that the toady, the hack
deserves a memorial.

The networks, the agencies
haven't kept us informed.
It's a queerer trade still
when our hypocrite doubles
write us cliff-hanging.

I'll take my pay, too,
now we are fellow citizens,
fellow exiles. Welcome,
one way or another, to
Nova Dacia. Pax.

>Note: Adrian Paunescu was the official poet of Ceausescu's Romania, which was once the Roman province of Dacia, to which Ovid was exiled.

# Crash

The trackball judders.
The display rattles the screen.
Down past each lit window of the Exchange
what flutters cannot be read
aloud to the uninitiate.
No fireside oenomancy
saw this declension in the lees.

"Get out while you can"
is more in the nature of
kindly advice than imperative
while the addicts boot up
manic spreadsheets on their laptops
and laugh as the marina
acquires gaps like a row of Bosnian terraces.

In the tabloids life goes on
nobly. Under the gilt aluminium
coaching lamps the wine list is heavy.
Smart is the aim, the theory,
but after hours it comes down to
the usual, thanks. We promise ourselves
that tomorrow we shall read the signs.

# When the Saints Go Marching Out

*When the unbeliever asks about your
faith, take him to the church and show
him your icons*
                *—Eighth-century Russian saying*

*Give me back the Berlin Wall.
Give me Stalin and Saint Paul.
I've seen the future, baby. It is murder.*
                *—Leonard Cohen*

Sofya Andreyevna, born when the red day broke,
now 75, arthritic, lies on the floor
of the Church of the Annunciation, Zaluch'ye.
Basil, George, the Archangel Michael,
her name-saint Sophia and even
the Virgin in gold are gone from the wall.

"Painted by Rublev himself" the village knew.
"After the style of ..." art historians
almost concurred. In due time
at Christie's or Sotheby's someone will decide.
The market will give them a real value.
For half a millennium they warded off
the wolves of doubt and reason.

*Multiple fractures to the skull
caused by repeated blows with a heavy object.*

Blood and hair on the silver candlestick
found in the snow by the fresh tyre tracks.

Sofya Andreyevna will survive
and in the few years left, remembering
siege, lack, terror, ice, will know
that none of them was strong enough to rip
her faith away like this.

# Love Poem for Stephanie

When we talk it should be
in Cocoliche or Baracoon,
some creole we can live in,
built from the tentative pidgin
of cultures touching lightly
like trade, like skin, learning
each other, working past
getting and giving to love.

When we move there should be
strange names for what we do
towards each other. No dance,
gambit or skater's leap
is new enough to make
such unnatural demands
on the lexicon of contact
and release, trust and surprise.

# Poem for Port Arthur

... where the cricket ground still shines like a brass thingummy
on an eager ensign's jacket
and muslin waves lap irony at the stone.
Diana never came here, but it doesn't matter.
By '96 romantic stories had long given way
to Convict Barbie and the Pentax Penitentiary.
This is a history of the urge to make a quid
and its consequences. Alf Maule would tap
with his walking stick *the very spot* on the flags
which a deed apocryphal even to Marcus Clarke
had stained. Alf and the other guides had the patter
as glib as a politician's response to massacre.
One of them, Jim MacArthur, had burned down the church
then made a living describing its remains.

Interpretation has always been the problem.
No wonder, when the press needed to doctor
electronically the killer's eyes. As if
the memory of picnic outings by steamer
for charitable causes wasn't enough.

Sunlight on the green or the weather off Cape Raoul
huge as empire: we still deny it all,
waiting for the next *son et lumière*, which will descend
like a princess.

# The Holy Tomato of Huddersfield

All she wanted was a sandwich for her school lunch
and she got God instead.
Shasta Aslam, 14, of Huddersfield
(as they put it in the papers)
sliced a tomato one ordinary morning
and the pattern of the pips spelled out,
clearly in arabic script, right to left:
"There is no god but Allah."
then, a line below: "Mohammed is the Messenger."

For centuries learned men will grapple
with the big theological question:
"How do you determine the right side of a tomato?"
while pilgrims to Huddersfield plead
with Shasta's heirs to open the freezer door
for just a second.

History will record she had to settle for a cinnamon bun
that holy day.

# Chronicles of the King

## 1. Esau Smith

They reckon Jesse Presley died at birth
but, fact is, one twin was enough
and old Aunt Reenie raised him down in Belden,
ten miles from Tupelo.
She bought both kids toy guitars from Sears
Christmas '45, gave Jesse
a ten buck note and a bible when he hit the road
at age fourteen to live on
vanilla cookies and Camels under the pier
at Pascagoula.

Working on the platforms at Hattiesburg,
moonlighting a bottle club out near
the Okatoma turn-off, in '53
Jesse cut "Bosom Divine"
with Jo-Jo Fineaux and His Hattiesburg Hepcats,
sold maybe a dozen copies,
then got to taking numbers, wound up in New Orleans,
heard his brother on the radio,
"Milkcow Blues Boogie", filled the payphone
with nickels calling Aunt Reenie.

She told him of the story
his daddy was spreading.
Right after that, Jesse got pinched
taking the single action,
did three months, came out
to no messages, changed his name,
well, he'd had time to read that old Bible,
found Esau, kept his nose clean,
got a job at a fancy joint on Carrollton,
dealing, push goes to the house.

Moved out West, just plain Smitty,
runs a bar, wife and two kids,
ain't getting any younger,
but still alive.


## 2. Apparition

Some time in the early sixties
Elvis was driving across the Texas Panhandle
along with Larry Geller, his hair stylist/guru,
on his way to Hollywood to make
yet another of those Hal Wallis crap movies
that it was trendy once to pretend to like
(he hated flying)
when they both looked up
and there in the big Texan sky
(in the heavens, if you will)
was a cloud in the exact form
of the face of Stalin.
No sooner had they mentioned this to each other
than a thunderbolt shot out of the cloud
narrowly missing their bus.

How does this fit in the greater scheme of things?
How does it compare
with the holy tomato of Huddersfield*,
the Mother Teresa cinnamon bun,
or, more importantly, with the hundreds
of recorded apparitions of Elvis's face
on tortillas all over the Southwest?
Why, you may ask, did the lightning miss?
Or how good a hair stylist did you have to be
(forgetting, for the moment, the guru bit)?
There are so many unanswered questions.

*See above p.9.

Stalin, of course, never saw Elvis in a vision
or, if he had, he never mentioned it
and had the hair stylist/apparatchik removed.
The chronology was wrong, but 1956
had been the year of Krushchev's biggest hit
and also of "Don't be Cruel".

Who was trying to tell whom what?
And am I being curmudgeonly to suggest
that it would be piss-weak by comparison
if Eminem saw Saddam in the clouds,
or even Kim Jong Il, who actually has
all those Hal Wallis movies on video?

## 3. EP for VP?

In '72 the Republicans wanted Elvis to run for VP.
Nixon figured it was cheaper than paying the fee Colonel Tom
                                                                           demanded
for a White House appearance.
And he'd have him around for longer.
What's more, he was straighter than Agnew, smarter than Ford,
and he sure as heck would have given Jimmy Carter a run in '76.
Nixon in the end settled for making the King a federal narcotics agent.

What prescience that much maligned
little ex-Quaker rat had! What insight!
We all put Nixon down just because
he was a cheat, a liar, a foul-mouthed megalomaniac,
a hypocrite, a warmonger, a blackguard,
a malefactor, a slippery, ignominious villain,
an immoral sink of roguery, a slurry of foul scum,
degenerate and totally without virtue.

But credit where it's due and against this
you have to admit the man was a genius.
Elvis as a narc! In one stroke so many problems solved.

I had always thought of him as a non-voting Democrat,
but, more important, he was youthful rebellion:
Paul Revere with voice and hips.
Stars and stripes and a twinkle in the eye,
The King of the Republic could crusade
against pharmaceutical evil,
could save a generation from the clutches
of freelance pushers, make the streets safe
for CIA approved smack and get
what he needed himself on the side.

Sort of 'You scratch my poison ivy and I'll scratch yours.'


## 4. There Will be Peace in the Valley for Me

> *Angels fly because they take themselves so lightly.*
> *– the King's last words*

When I die, I want to go with a cliché on my lips,
preferably New Age nuanced.
How do you prepare for death?
By hedging your bets, by having
a Greek Orthodox doctor, a Jewish dentist
and ecumenical jewellery?

The Elvis Presley Memorial Trauma Centre still works,
but the King's name was removed
from the plaque at the *Arizona* memorial,
Pearl Harbour, despite $52,000.
Was a girlfriend called Shirley Dieu help
or hindrance?

Of course, he was too early to join
the First Presbyterian Church of the Divine Elvis
or to worship at his own weeping statue
owned by Toon Nieuwenhuisen,
impersonator and disciple.

All impersonators are disciples in a way,
especially Elvis Singh, who created the lines,
"I don't do drugs, I don't do bourbon.
All I want to do is shake my turban."

The first man to photograph the King
was the same Barrett (first name unrecorded)
who took the autopsy shots of the Roswell aliens
and has since disappeared.
Did that camera steal Elvis's soul?
And does that explain the restlessness
resulting in all those sightings?

When the time comes, when the last strain
to shit proves too much for the heart
and I tumble fom the bog seat, dropping my copy
(only half-read) of *The Holy Shroud of Turin*,
what will I have to offer when I stand
before the Pearly Box Office?
Just this: "I was more than a fan.
I lived only to imitate."

# Aerodynamics

The field where Wittgenstein flew his kites
behind The Grouse, high above sheep
and Glossop, is now a helipad.
He would have understood the use
of the tourism text, even though the rotors
in chopping the traces of clear currents
are not there, as I am, in homage
to clear thought. Views of the Peak District,
thirty quid a spin, stranded hikers
lifted from ontology and snow.

Ah, the kites, the winds of Kant, the answer
blowing on the moors!

Theory trudges in to The Grouse's snug
and orders a pint of Thwaites.
Doctrine and method foam together
while the sleet drives in from Heptonstall
across the bitter valley, across
the kiteless black air from Sylvia's grave
where language functions on a simple card,
anonymous: "With love" in a small hand.
Beyond logical necessity, the absence of kites
flies like a tautology screaming in the gale.

Below the weather commerce scrawls
propositions between mills and learning.
Love and stone wear each other. Words
bear all our kites and shape our air.

# Speaking for Myself

*i.m. Brett Whiteley*

You gave me the American Dream
I had already been dreaming,
portraits of shared heroes,
dared lines, sweet games.

You drowned me through the ultramarine
of my harbour, exploded me
—palm tree or lion—terrible
as brain, river, sex, flight, self.

You took my addictions,
curved them into your blood,
swirled mushroom waves, the beaks
and hills, the alchemy of need.

Now I have to see round corners
for myself. What I see
is the full warm promise
of an empty motel room,

the air and debris fidgeting
with infinity, the trick perfumed
and sacred, waiting. I hang between
redemption's con and courage.

# ... and a Pound of Round

Taking the festival posters around,
went into the butcher's shop in the Quadrant.
The old guy came up to the counter.

"Poetry eh?
Had a bloke in the shop the other day
talking about poetry
I told him: 'Shakespeare,
Shakespeare's the best poet there ever was.'
He said to me, 'What about Wordsworth, eh?'
'Wordsworth? He was English wasn't he?'
The one I always like is that feller
Mansfield. You know:
'I must go down to the seas again.'
That one comes to me mind
every time I go down to the beach
at night like. Yeah
I do a bit of fishin'.
'The lonely sea and the sky.'
Yeah. That'd be my favourite.
Course you can put a poster on the door."

# The Aisles

> *In Greece, he'd sing some sort of hymn like this t' ye:*
> —*Byron, Don Juan, Canto III*

The poets and postcards were right.
The Aegean is as blue as Toilet Duck,
but I wouldn't drink wine that shade of dark.

On Hydra, "le Johnston de nos jours",
I soak up my own light aura of pretension
along with the retsina splashed by sun

and play at being the poet playing at
being the tourist. This is by way of
a snapshot greeting from the isles

where burning Byron ... and you know the rest,
including the history of the one island
which consistently sold out,

to the Venetians, the Turks and now the Yanks.
And Karamanlis died today,
le Menzies de leurs jours.

So I drink at the Sun Set Bar
halfway between Disco Heaven
and the yacht club's bikinis

and watch the wakes, like chips of temple marble,
slice neat as Visa cards across the path
of Phoebus plunging with his dazzling trolley.

"Yet in these times he might have done much worse:"
George's irony was less cliff than balcony.
The view's still clear, the octopus delicious.

# The Living Are Left with Imagined Lives

*i.m. Robert Harris*

You will not add age's load to wisdom's.
It would have been superfluous, anyway,
best left for those who need a longer lease.
You carried, you said, the sins of the city
on your shoulders, no bed or desk so awkward
that the lies it had produced could not be straightened
round the narrowest stair-turnings of the heart.

So much that hasn't died sings darkly:
Piaf's hollow bones as flutes for fire,
each albatross rigging the clouds with wit,
the sweat and comity of useful work,
scraps of sad Jane wherever light meets stone,
but, mostly, love tough as the skin on old words
yet still too slippery for the nets
the honest eclipse has dropped between us.

"A million golden birds of future vigor"
you wished me once. What skies of mine they've graced
have been the more open for the memory
of your discourse, its hard innocence,
of courage lacking calculation,
your blunt face butting at the truth.

# Suter Hartmann & Rahtjen's Composition Co. Ltd

The light and shadow on the
flanks of the super-dreadnought in the
Red Hand Brand poster on the
wall might be only through the
window, or it might be real,
having been put there by the
original artist.

And the weather, too,
that grey in the distance—
rain clouds or smog?
Admiralty Floating Dock
or White Bay?

What failure of prevailing wind will
leave it heavy over
the painters, dockers?

Antifouling paint
is the medium to use in this harbour.

# ... and a Pound of Round

Taking the festival posters around,
went into the butcher's shop in the Quadrant.
The old guy came up to the counter.

"Poetry eh?
Had a bloke in the shop the other day
talking about poetry
I told him: 'Shakespeare,
Shakespeare's the best poet there ever was.'
He said to me, 'What about Wordsworth, eh?'
'Wordsworth? He was English wasn't he?'
The one I always like is that feller
Mansfield. You know:
'I must go down to the seas again.'
That one comes to me mind
every time I go down to the beach
at night like. Yeah
I do a bit of fishin'.
'The lonely sea and the sky.'
Yeah. That'd be my favourite.
Course you can put a poster on the door."

# The Aisles

> *In Greece, he'd sing some sort of hymn like this t' ye:*
> —*Byron, Don Juan, Canto III*

The poets and postcards were right.
The Aegean is as blue as Toilet Duck,
but I wouldn't drink wine that shade of dark.

On Hydra, "le Johnston de nos jours",
I soak up my own light aura of pretension
along with the retsina splashed by sun

and play at being the poet playing at
being the tourist. This is by way of
a snapshot greeting from the isles

where burning Byron ... and you know the rest,
including the history of the one island
which consistently sold out,

to the Venetians, the Turks and now the Yanks.
And Karamanlis died today,
le Menzies de leurs jours.

So I drink at the Sun Set Bar
halfway between Disco Heaven
and the yacht club's bikinis

and watch the wakes, like chips of temple marble,
slice neat as Visa cards across the path
of Phoebus plunging with his dazzling trolley.

"Yet in these times he might have done much worse:"
George's irony was less cliff than balcony.
The view's still clear, the octopus delicious.

Liberation's not a phallic ruin,
a flag-stripe against the sky,
a flush of azure on the porcelain.

The world's shelves are wiped
clean as sunlight. They are stocked
with meditations on antiquity.

# Love Poem (Dental)

Let me suck the strands of meat
from between your teeth—mussel, chicken, rump;
ours is a well-fed love. I want to be
like one of those birds you see on TV documentaries,
part vulture, part floss,
but most of all part
of the grand ecological design—
planet by Greenaway or Telemann.
Does this make me a conductor in the food chain?
Architect sounds too grand, too much like
the Swiss watch parables from Sunday School:
"How to confute an atheist".
I don't want to confute you, darling;
confuse, maybe, all sorts of verbs
beginning with 'con-', but mostly
I want to contribute
to your oral hygiene. Your breath so sweet
I want to sweeten even more
than any '50s pop lyric, '60s slogan or '70s waistcoat,
more than the honeyed greed of that best forgotten decade,
more even than the saccharine smell of Iraq burning
its way into the New World Order.
A millennial sweetness will blast
like something from Revelations, Revlon or Reveille,
and it will set the world's teeth on edge,
but yours will be whiter, sharper,
all the better to graze lightly and teasingly
over the surface of whatever you fancy.

# Tens

Another ten, luv?
    Yeah, another ten
        and a sideways glance

at the pub's logo
    curled like a smile
        across her T-shirt

and the Sky Channel odds
    are getting shorter
        and louder

and another ten
    slapped from the tap
        with more head

than I'll be getting
    tonight in a
        strange town

and the third at Doomben
    high above the pool table
        slams someone's hopes.

Another ten, luv
    and a packet of nuts
        and a glance held longer

and the change
    glints from its puddle
        on the bar,

the black ball thunks
    and the favourite
        wins the next.

I drain the last ten,
    pocket the change.
        The car park's cold.

# Cold War

The forties, that avuncular decade:
Not only Joe and Walt, one at each shoulder,
but all those other uncles back from the war that took fathers,
lounging by motor-cars in wide-trousered suits,
the childless ones that always swung you highest,
the slightly fabulous, the mildly crude,
the one who could fart the "Reveille"
and the slim, worried one with a face
firm and smooth as a cigarette from an art deco pack.

There were aunts, of course, and cousins
who were never quite as real as neighbour kids.

But it was the uncles who were in tune
with the years of Hoagie and Bogie,
of boogie and childish hunting, hiding games.

# Coming Apart at the Scene

*for Alison Symes*

With a shoe full of blood
the poets arrive,
drive over the bridge
and lose the library.

Wrong car park,
wrong decade,
right building,
wrong floor.

Leave the shoe full of blood
in the back of the hire car.

Walk barefoot into the office
of the Department of Mining, Construction,
Energy, Resources, Industry, Finance and the Arts.
"The library's upstairs."
"Where's the stairs?"
"There aren't any."
"Lift?" "No lift."
You can get there,
but not from here.

Figures. Sort of like heaven.
No short cuts for bureaucrats.

So it's back out,
limp and wince
across the car park,
up to where the books are,
where flowers are being given
and a choir is singing.

# Brontë Country

I swear I saw Branwell, young again,
in a pub in Haworth through the karaoke crowd.
I remembered Doris Leadbetter's story of the village drunk
who sat in the corner "an' Branwell were the village drunk before me
an' this were 'is chair." This dark-curled American tourist, all Pre-
                                    Raphaelite
and solitary with his bitter, not playing the pokies and definitely not
looking at the historical prints of railway scenes as monochrome as
                                    the skyline,
TV antennae and all, on a day no brighter than the parsonage,
sat, still as the couch on which Emily died but better preserved,
his eyes the colour of the tumbling gravestones up on the hill
or the shadows that hide, waiting for the sunlight
when they will skid like fictitious siblings,
a source of visible delight
but unneccesary.

# Animal, Medical or Visceral

Is it found in the toy cupboard at playgroup?
Does it have opposing thumbs?
When you squeeze it, does it play Rachmaninov?
Is it bigger than a tutti frutti jelly belly?
Smaller than a Denver Broncos tight end?
Did it ever have a bit part in a Jim Jarmusch movie?
Was it in Dodi's Mercedes just before the tunnel?
Has it been impounded by Customs, the Vice Squad or the RSPCA?
When you say "yes", do you mean all of them?
Does it turn blue when you look away from it?
Is it known to frequent university libraries?
Renal dialysis units?
The lingerie counter at Harris Scarfe?
Can it swim underwater for more than 50 metres?
Did Helen Darville ever claim to be it?
Did it refuse to join Heaven's Gate, but regret the decision after they
                                        went off in the spaceship?
After it won the Archibald Prize and the Caulfield Cup in the same
                            year, did it refuse to speak to the media?
Even to Triple J?
Does it own a collection of rare Barbie Dolls?
Does it wear a burkha in the backyard?
Do you realise that I've asked more than twenty questions?
Have you twigged that I worked it out after the fifth?
That was when you answered, "It depends which tight end you
                                                            mean."
I've been stringing you along ever since.
But I promise I'll keep it a secret, so you can use it in another game.

# The Training of the Urban Guerrilla

*after Marighela*

Apart from technical preparation,
other useful forms of training are
hiking, camping and spending long periods in rough country,
mountain-climbing, swimming, canoeing,
deep-sea diving and fishing
(as practised by frogmen),
fishing, shooting birds and catching game.

It is important to know how to
drive a car, pilot a plane,
handle both motor- and sailing-boats,
to know something of
mechanics, radio, telephones
and even electronics.

It is equally important to know
something of topography,
to know how to locate one's position,
to calculate distances,
to make maps and plans,
to measure time, transmit messages,
use a compass and so on.

A knowledge of chemistry,
of colour-combinations,
the ability to make rubber stamps
and imitate other people's handwriting:
these and other skills are part of
the urban guerrilla's technical training.
If he is to survive
in the society he wants to destroy,
he must be able to forge documents.

When it comes to medical care,
the guerrilla must have skills equivalent
to those of doctors, nurses and pharmacists
in order to prescribe and use medicines
and perform surgery.

The most important element, however,
remains that of handling such weapons as
sub-machine guns
revolvers
automatics
mortars
bazookas
FAL guns
and other types of carbine
as well as a knowledge of the various kinds of
ammunition and explosives.
Dynamite is one instance.
It is also vital to know how to use
incendiary bombs
smoke bombs
Molotov cocktails
tear gas
mines
and grenades;
also to make and repair weapons
to destroy bridges
dislodge or destroy
railway lines and sleepers.

The urban guerrilla will complete his training
in a specially organised technical centre,
but only after being tested in action,
having actually fought the enemy.

Some guerrillas have weakened
and disappeared or resigned.

# Don Gibson and Etymology

The other night, listening to "Sea of Heartbreak",
I picked up on the word "caress".
It is, of course, cognate with
"charity" and "whore" and the Latvian
*kars*, meaning "randy".

                "Memories of ..."
fingernails light on the lower back,
the Smith Family building set among
Joe Borg's brothels—East Sydney '68.

"... so divine." Well, a good ol'
C & W boy can be excused
for confusing the divine
with the desirable.

                The song
goes on: "How I wish ... "
I'm on dry land, on a mountain,
in a room full of dictionaries.
Cars are for driving, for ferrying across water,
and no-one speaks Latvian any more.

# Relaxed and Comfortable

Tasmania's losing its democracy, but it still retains
its four seasons: roo, deer, duck and possum.
We're leasing the wires but we're giving away the polls;
they're 40 per cent too expensive.

I don't want to be part of a Nation, whether it is One
or whether it has a leader who can count even beyond that.
I just want to live here, a not too innocent bystander,
standing at short leg to the globalised spin doctors:

a sort of David Boon of the level playing field,
while ATMs chew up the bush as if it was a dodgy card
and call centres are calling you-oo-oo-hoo-oo-oo-hoo,
but when you fly into Sydney business class

the harbour looks even bluer than how Brett painted it
and the high-rises, when the sun is at a happy angle,
are as clean and relevant as a Tandberg cartoon,
an Iron Pot Bay chardonnay or a Matthew Richardson mark.

Meanwhile, if God had meant us to be compassionate
It wouldn't have given us the stock exchange
and if It'd meant us to be serious
It wouldn't have invented the Hollywood Argyles.

There is nowhere better than a relaxed and comfortable possie
(unless it be a tired and emotional one)
from which to look into the face of the future,
which was last observed behind a balaclava on Webb Dock.

# Massive Quartzes

Aventurine, golden or greenish spangled
due to small inclusions of mica.
The matrix is brownish
and a metallic sheen is produced
by the inclusions.
There are two varieties:
/with inclusions of chrome-mica (green)/
/with inclusions consisting of
small flakes of ferric oxide (red)/

Quartz cat's eye, pale brown,
enclosing light-coloured fibrous asbestos
(mineralogically an amphibole asbestos).
When cut en cabochon it produces
a typically undulating light reflection
known as a "chatoyant" effect.
Quartz cat's eye does not have
the opalescence of true cat's eye
(cymophane chrysoberyl).

Tiger's eye, identical in structure
to cat's eye, but chatoyant
through intrusions of crocidolite
oxidised to a golden brown.

Prase, a fibrous quartz,
the included fibres being
actinolite (a green amphibole)
giving the stone a leek-green colour.

Falcon's eye, sapphire quartz
and amethyst quartz:
varieties with inclusions
of blue or purple
unoxidised crocidolite.

Rose quartz, coarsely granular,
pale pink, often cloudy.
Its pleochroism whitish and rose red.
Asterism is well seen
in stones cut semispherical.

# Erechtheus 33's Apologia

*for Mark Davis*

I posted my modernism by snail-mail, dropped it in
the humanist slot in the box that didn't have
E II R on it any more. Gough mit uns.
It was addressed "Dear Reader", an anagram for
er, er, er, Dada. Iconoclasm
is being smashed again. I never got around
to buying a TV. Gilligan's Island
was more remote than Santa Catalano,
"26 miles across the sea". A bunch
of Bradys that didn't include Matt
or Veronica might as well have been
the Mangoplah-Cookardinia United
half-back line or the offspring of
the drover's wife and the drover's dog.

Now they say Ern Malley and Detective Vogelesang
were on the same team. Cultural theory,
conspiracy theory: someone's not
the full denko and it might well be me.
The absence of Martin Bryant jokes tells us
that the line is always drawn somewhere,
but by whom? Gatekeepers, drunken porters—
Hal, Peter, Dorothy or Prêt à—
"Eat up your whalemeat and don't blubber
about the El Niño effect, the Sal Mineo effect
or how green is Green Valley," they still warn me.
When I was an Argonaut I never got
a Blue Certificate and I never quite made it
as a bodgie. Can I join your gang?

# Knowing Your Place

"In my day cleaners knew their place."
But she didn't tell me where that was,
or which day was hers. Perhaps
it was when we were told to hide.

"During changeover the best place to be
is in your room." Or else the kids
might, glancing as they stampede class
to class, notice an adult who seems

not linked to learning's paper-chain:
homework, exams, diplomas, pay-slips—
and be confused, might even think
there's more to school than they were taught.

Worse, they might twig that shiny floors,
clear windows, walls you don't stick to,
germ-free loos don't just happen
at the Principal's decree.

In her day? To all appearances
she's still alive, so surely this
is her day too, today when we
no longer cower with the mops.

We've always known our place. We've known
the art-room clay intimately, in our lungs.
We've known the gobs of phlegm on handrails,
the benchtops' sick explicit words.

Next time she comes that line I'll ask her,
"Which place was that? Was it marked
on some map by the coffee ring left
by a staff-room cup, and did I wipe it off?"

# Weeding my Grandparents' Grave

Summergrass, fat hen, flatweeds mostly,
grey-green against the en-tout-cas
that bounces tennis-ball memories back
across the net of names and dates
to when the world was being born for me
and black marble was portentous, not slick.

But one whitened spike of a dead weed
more woody than the rest stood up
at a cocky angle, as odd here as my lobbing
after 35 years, priapic in the middle
of a king-sized-bed-sized tomb, patrilinear
as the tradition in this safe family.

A vegemite jar half-full of pebbles
must have held the artificial flowers
we have always preferred to mess,
but which of my scattered cousins (whom
I barely know) placed it there? The traces
of glue where the label was have almost gone.

I cross the road to break off a piece
of wattle, grab a few pink and purple
weeds that were announcing spring in some
haphazard way between the plots
and do a tasteful arrangement, shoot a snap
which no-one else will want to see.

The season's really too far gone for wattle.
The road I've run across was where
I once fell out of the car after visiting them.
I bled all over Mother's best frock
as she held me in the front seat
of the Prefect the rest of the way home.

# These Days You Need All the Work You Can Get

The dark-complexioned bloke on the righ
sells scratchies down at the newsag
and moonlights
on Fr
exc

The blonde midwife
slips out of the room
to put a bra on.
Things are getting that seriou
She's better kno n as
            ing.
         lous,

The celebrant is al
a TV weather girl part-ti

      followed by
christmas pudding fl  ured ice-cr

       nd fat Lisa
punches Brett on the should
when he goes too fa

Caught without a notepad,
the ALP candidate
jots this d n in biro
between t e columns
of a grease-blotched *Woman's Day*,
wh   s why ther  re
some patches missing.

# At Table

*i.m. Gwen Harwood*

Aperitifs and antipasto
bring talk of weather, friends and work.
The consommé's as rich as music.
Arias of conversation
slip, *glissando*, round the room.

*Miss Foster's no longer in the office.*
Perched no longer on her desk,
she's flying through these soft exchanges.
As the table's cleared for entrée
the topic turns to literature.

Mutability *in situ*:
red replaces chardonnay.
Russell, Wittgenstein and Ayer,
epistemology and how
to live; the main course is consumed.

Yet change implies something's remembered.
Light as a playful sorbet, words
are strong, not just to cleanse and sweeten.
Time is a tongue that's hinged and mobile.
The softest palate's backed by bone.

Layer after layer's vanished.
No-one's at the table now.
Night's as black as bitter coffee.
*Miss Foster's no longer in the office.*
They never could keep track of her.

# Keeping the Dream Alive

The place is full of jealous whingers
who want to cut down the tallest poppy
in the trade. Together we can pull through this,
mate. Maaaateship. I love to have a beer with Lawsy, 'cos ...
There's too many of you out there
not pulling your weight, not game enough
to get behind the banks.
You've gotta be game, game as ...
Does Westpac still have a branch at Jerilderie?
Talk back to an ATM with a seven second delay,
which is longer than it took for Ned to say
"Such is life" or Red Barry to gong him
off *Hey Hey It's the Nineteenth Century.*

And I say this, Australia:
If we don't all, in the best Aussie tradition,
get in there and pass the hat round for the shareholders
of our great financial institutions,
there's no hope for us as a decent nation
and the shooting of Sergeant Kennedy at Stringybark Creek
might just as well have been any other Kennedy death.
Sid Nolan's paintings will be lined up against the wall and hung
then sold for $1.2 million
and whose vault will it be that they go into?
Ah, Snowtown, heart of Australia, where they keep
the welfare bludgers off the streets
with a little help from the ANZ
and a little help from the NAB
and the Commonwealth,
because wealth is so common
that you and I, Australia, can afford to watch it,
our greatest spectator sport since public executions.

# Et in Acadia Ego?

## 1. Bob Harris Real Estate, Cole Harbour NS

So should all the best poets be reincarnated.
Signs all over Eastern Nova Scotia
show that this time around
Bob is selling heaven in quarter-acre lots:
tiny islands with spruce grove and rowboat,
white clapboard house with red barn
and view of the Atlantic through mist
by a bream-glinting inlet
where two old men and a small girl
fish from the bridge for a whole tide
and don't mind not catching anything.
What's more, this time around
Bob's getting his fair cut.

## 2. Forbes, Dr John (G.P.) New Glasgow NS

Here's karmic reward for a healer of the mind,
and the pay's better: allergies, infections,
kids' tummyaches, certificates for sickies –
and there's plenty of those at the steelworks,
the paper mills, the Pioneer mine where the strike is two months
                                                                                                        long
and Bill Guthro was run into a ditch last Thursday
by a company front-end loader.
I know John'll fix him up as he fixed us all.
Dispensing jovial wisdom in a small town
must be a cinch after being a Sydney boy
trying to pick winners in compassionate Melbourne.

## 3. Salmon River Presbyterian Church. Minister: Rev. Andrew Hardy

Having refused, eloquently, to preach in Launceston
but having guided us over the city rooftops
and along the stencilled walls of wit
now the "defender of family values"
can strike a pose as snowy and neo-Gothic
as his wooden church and command
the respect denied tagless graffitists
and self-published poets no matter how
much genius is squeezed into the casual smile.
Thinking long and connected no longer,
let us pray. This, after all, is the next life.

# "… good grammar / and an unclouded eye…"

*for Dimitris Tsaloumas*

That's what was needed
not only for the odyssey
but for the log of it, for tone-pure charts
that others, readers or surfers,
might marvel at while roaring with sun
through everything that washes in
where bronzed Bondi previews
the arid sands, the centre. History,
rather like "values", just squats there
waiting for tourists, amateur archaeologists.

Meanwhile, Dimitris, water cavorts at
your cragged stanzas and you look out
and away, refusing the soft fear
that shifts and covers, grains too fine
to build with, too silky to dig.

There is a severity beyond the reach
of lifesavers, out where the ocean is
as accurate as any of your songs
and as deep.

# Mother and Son

It's March again, our month. Now
it's a different hospital, a different city.
We talk above the nebuliser's roar:
part chainsaw, part surf, all edge.

The spasms of pain are at closer intervals
as you labor, this time to postpone
the separation. Your skin's cross-stitched
with butterflies and bruises.

Your hands, which I never heard play Poulenc,
never fast enough, you said,
grip, but mine keep slipping
as I slipped away from you those years ago.

Holding on isn't always everything. Skin slides.
Too tough to die, too proud to call this living,
you hug into these punctuated hours
our missed half-century of love.

# For my Father

My friends are writing elegies for their fathers.
I have so much to say about you, and memories
have nothing to do with it. We never met.
You have conned me even more effectively
than all your other gulls and marks.
You conned me into being. Forty years
I held you dead hero or at least Kilroy.

Then when you really died I became
your ghost. Your hairline, chin and gait
returned to haunt those who barely mourned,
while you still con me and I fall for it
again, giving you life.

                      No doubt you wore
the Flying Officer's uniform more dashingly
the night you conned my mother than I wear
your face and limbs. Nothing I have written
has had a punchline half as sharp
as Grandmother's signature when you put it
on your prize fiction work, her will.

Did you ever imagine my fantasies,
and was that why you had all those medals
no-one ever won who never left
Sale or Laverton except on leave or awol?
We picked the same *Boys' Own* stories
to not grow out of.

                 Once I wrote,
"Seeking heroics, we become absurd."
But that was about me. You found heroics
easy as any pose: judge, doctor, engineer.
Post-modern before your time, you had

more style than Walter Mitty. Once you shaped up
against an angry neighbour who had inches,
stone and skill on you. He backed away.

I've swapped audacity for irony.
You never pretended to be
anything less than excellent.
No wonder you could not acknowledge me.

# Meditation on Parliament House, Canberra, 2002

Among the free world's lesser bastions
it would be easy to miss this minor
bunker under the rammed earth, the sheepish
grass, where the descendants of Macarthur's
Spanish/South African mindless ovines
cringe still, waiting for the fleecing, the dip
and drench, the indignity of the dogs
yapping and yarding, the orders to jump,
if it were not for the sheet of flag, flat
against a sky too torpid even to
galvanise irony, a standard that
proclaims: "It is night in the motherland;
the stars are out against the deep blue;
they surround the flag that comforts, blankets.
Sleep and dream of super japes in Iraq."

And the sheep toss only lightly, aware
that the Bush is vastly empty, a void
of inanity more terrifying
even than their own inbred Merino
aristocratic blankness, pure and white.

# Dry

"Bleached" grass (by some white king of science?)
or "blanched"? but anyway a fire hazard,
if hazard is not too tentative a word in February
for the pale invasive culture
we have introduced, will, if chance
roots among the shiny bulblets,
catch.

We hold as lightly as death
the living topsoil and hardly
the rock, but we are very good
with surfaces and glyphosate.

What is left to walk through,
however delicately placed each
of our RM Williams boots?
What you see. Every look kills.
Blind hazard, accidental sight
burn as much as they smother.

I think "blanching" (as if with fear, yet slightly active)
but I dare not be sure.

If I think like this summer hillside
what white distortions will I undergo?
Easier to ask, "What is to be done?"
(The passive either a cop-out
or hypocrisy) than to gamble
with answers in the onion twitch.

# Zig-Zag Track

*for CA Cranston*

Go lightly on the dolerite.
Only a leap away from the lookout bedrock is
lower than sea level.
Where the high voltage wires
start across the gorge
the sign reads "instant death".
These days no-one takes the time to decay slowly
the way the rock forms soil.

The jointing pattern jumps from point to
point. From she-oak to native hop,
geniculate and furcular, difficult
as speech, simple as lines of air,
the cracks write no warning.
What Jurassic texts we might read
are translated by guess and mostly we start
from the scratch of nervous energy,
the need to mark, to sign:
"instant death", "be warned",
"here be ..."

Electric and delicate, death
will click into place.

# Scapeland

What did I see, 495.4 m above the estuary?
Not the encrusted life on the oyster shell,
not a single dotterel headfeather, nor even
the sheen of the shard of a curlew's egg.
I was too high to discern
individual strands of kelp or shopping bags.

The freeway stretched like a campaign ribbon
on the soft barathea breast of a uniform
beneath which the heart of a general
who loved his grandchildren and kept fit beat.
I saw the chilled cubes of apartment buildings
with names stolen from California and palm trees
hijacked from the comfort of deserts.

The water in sunlight gleamed
like a brand new digital camera making a frame,
finding the view, metering the light, creating art.

The land shaft, the Apex lookout like
a land ship: what price etymology?
How gilt is language's frame where
we choose what to overlook, what to blame?

# Writing the World

Metaphor's glib: the poem as ...
suicide bomber, detainee,
wild river. The problem always
to live the meaning, when to write
only is at best to catalogue
or preach, cop out at worst.

How to mean the land?
As stones and currawongs
write, as 80 grand a year
buys dissertations on texts
no laptop ever shone,
where does creating fit?

Beyond taxonomy, beyond
marketable terror,
honesty always lies
somewhere over the line.
Flying is facile. Walk,
roll, crawl beyond the pale.

Make a mark. Leave no sign
unturned. Carry your baggage out.
Avoid the easy paradox
and give no orders.
Respect what you re-use
and sing innocently.

In weather that would turn milk,
when waiting uses all strength,
take the estuary's voice
and the sour clouds' script;
be a consultant to the air,
amanuensis to the earth.

# aUStralia

## the recent history of a small continent in 22 poems

# Oosutoraria

> ... *in the whole world there is not a worse country*
> —*Major Robert Ross, 1788*
> ...*the kokakoala bear / for mascot*...
> —*Selwyn Pritchard, 2000*

So nature's arse-about. It has to be
where birds are blood-bright for camouflage
among the deeds and trophies the National Trust
and National Party hallow. The black swan
of impasse has its season now and then,
is vice-regally shot, Game's game, anyone's cur
for the price of a drink. Our heritage:
the sailors of the *Sydney* who sang like kangaroos,
Pearce's Lewis gun detachment, defeated
by a platoon of emus in '32, out West.
Now that the Lion has lain down with the Lam-
borghini the fauna can stand proud
with cultural identity, Mickey and Minnie
by the plagueful, Easter Bunnies enough
to turn the paddocks the colour of milk chocolate,
and natives, too, the scissor-wielding dingo
of Uluru, a six-pack of fairy penguins
(easier to carry), on Rottnest a game
of quokka soccer. When the thylacine
smiles now we know it's not only because
the brewery got its tail wrong on the labels.

Progress is not passé, even in Adelaide.
By the end of the decade no headland
will be without a concrete toilet block.
New tar shouts on the road like Texan wealth
all the way to Jewel. On the box
smiles are tight lycra and, look again,

those aren't tears but sweat drops
as the steroid republic pumps its way
to the starting block. If you're sent off
for snarling "bloody Mabo" to the ref
you can always appeal. Just remember
to hold the akubra more or less over
your heart when they play anything by Peter Allen
as you blink at the top of the flagpole.

No smartarse mentions angst down at the Rissole.
Angst is a silent cliff, its vastness
easily swallowed by a shouldered Sony or the yawn
of a motel desk-clerk reading Laissez Murray
in the original English.

We remember every 25th of April
that Australia doesn't rhyme with success
and there's an autographed Fairlie Arrow poster
even in the Last Resort.

# Vinegar Hill

Across the Blue Mountains lay the fabled lands,
Tir na-n'Og and Hy Brasil, Mac Con Glinne's realm
where everything is made of food. The eternal West
of Celtic heaven called to the croppy boys in hell.

"Pikes, pikes! We'll plant the Liberty Pole
in King's garden, finish in New South Wales
what we started in Wexford, live forever!"
But General Holt preferred to lick English spittle.

So with Cunningham at Castle Hill
less than a thousand of "the most wild,
ignorant and savage Race" faced death
not liberty, but not before some fun.

They dragged the flogger, Duggan, out
from where he curled, squeaking, under his bed,
a mouse for the cat. "United Irishmen"
was a poor joke. The newly united kingdom

had more solidarity, had onside
the tired and the toadies, had the last laugh
when the lads ran up against Laycock,
who in his bright boots was six foot six

"and he could not get any higher as he took
blood money in England". Even the petty sycophant,
Ruse, "natef of Cornwall", stood too high,
while that long squirt of piety,

Marsden, over the triangle, under the flag,
his bible squat and dark as a rum bottle,
cast a shadow longer than a gun
on grass too wretched ever to be green.

# Pinchgut

Mattewanye had been a rock
of oysters and fun, sacred
to salt slitherings on picnics.
When the men in strange skins came,
their faces the colour of galahs,
they put a corpse up there, the dead flag
of a man called Morgan, who'd used
his cooper's hammer to tap into
half a pint of rum through someone's skull.

Flapping in chains it was meant as
a warning, was more an ensign.
Mattewanye has been boarded
by death and now sails on the harbour
under a sun that dries gunpowder
on water that tastes of gunpowder,
crewed by the doubly exiled
who starve there, guts pinched by salt.
Generations who'd slurped pleasure there
will never go back. It's fit for
a storehouse, a fort or a clock.

# Jonathan Burke McHugo Comes to Town

He sailed up the Tamar, a potentate
lolling on a settee on the poop deck.
Ever since the Indian sun had spiced
his brains too richly he'd had such fits,
believing himself royal. His crew
would humour him, make due obeisance.

The whole of Launceston turned out to watch
mad Jonathan disembark. It was a year
for madness, 1811: King George,
this "Count and Prince of the Blood", and Gordon,
sad crazy Gordon whose pate, too, had been
curried for the Empire and who'd ended up
Commandant of its foulest colony,
Launceston.

          Gordon greeted Jonathan,
who handed out madeira and advice
royally, explained his mission to reclaim
the island for the Crown (i.e. himself),
persuaded Gordon that he was to blame
for all the troubles of the settlement,
deserved jail. Gordon agreed. Power passed
from madman to madman. Dissent was drowned
in sweet wine or darkened by the shadow
of the gallows. For a week Jonathan ruled.

Lieutenant Lyttleton, young, passionate,
loyal and sane, freed a protesting Gordon,
manhandled Jonathan back to his brig,
tied him down and sailed him through the heads.
Launceston, some say, recovered.

# Phrenology

Where would we be without a knowledge
of the moral organs of the brain,
those subtle undulations of stuff
the consistency of good gruel or roe
that can leave their mark on bone?

Praise science that has shown us
how the skull preserves
the shape of good and evil
and how the native race
lacks the bumps of virtue.

We have collected thousands
of heads, removing the soft,
useless or perishable parts,
so as to get down to hard facts
and be sure of our findings.

We have also found an over-endowment
in the faculties of observation
compared to Englishmen.
Of course we sent the skulls
back home for precise measurement.

# Spider Dance and Horse Whip

> *The symbol of innocence is the statue of Eve*
> —*Lola Montez*

The dance had little to do with innocence
or statues, but we get the point.
Eve is what she makes you make of her.
Lola spun the miners tight and sticky,
danced her nocent web lightly, shaking
its strands till they dazzled like the vein
through the Gravel Pits or the lines
that join the silver stars of the flag.

Each small muscle under the satin
skin or fleshy silk could, flexing, suck
a man's brains out through his cock
at ten yards distance. Every part of her
could pout an invitation.

Innocence is winning a horse whip
in a raffle and joking about critics.
A whip can dance eight-legged, light
over a bug-eyed face, can weave
red webs as rapidly as any editor
can boil and spit out "notoriety".

To whip up a stockade against the traps
of the flesh, against the trapdoor predator,
is useless. Innocence is a tricky art.
It can be spun on stage and stretched
to catch a full house or to tangle
one man's anger and a town's lust.

# Bangar

George Macdonald, short, hunchbacked,
was known by the King's River mob
to be their loved dead Bangar "jumped up
again as a white man". For two years
they respected his new state, indulged
his appetites for curios and women.

When he left for Sydney the whole mob wept,
with "every epithet of endearment" begged him
not to go. He had jails to run, Armidale
to found, couldn't hang about in Port Macquarie
playing god when advancement called: Later
as Crown Lands Commissioner he ordered
the Grafton massacre. Gods exist
to mix love with justice. Sometimes
they get it wrong and a river chokes with limbs.

Sometimes it's better to stay put.

# Mandarin of the Crystal Button

The *Afghan* lay in Sydney Harbour, hundreds
of Chinese passengers below decks,
a few tense guards. After the torchlight march
of 5,000 from the Town Hall, fired
by Ninny Melville, Norton and grog,
had forced a note from Parkes that he would break
the law and keep them out—the birth
of the White Australia Policy that never was—
the press went on board and played their part
by telling the cops that the Chinese would eat them.

Quong Tart ate no-one but, like any other
British gentleman, he ate this land,
gorged on his Araluen Eldorado,
having arrived aged nine and skinny
on the fields, grew with the tea trade,
joined the Masons and the Oddfellows,
umpired at cricket, wore kilt and sporran.
"I never thought Lord Carrington
was so dark complexioned," someone said
on seeing him with other dignitaries.

Quong Tart went on board the *Afghan*,
worked a deal over a cuppa,
kept everyone sweet (enough to eat),
said later, "I like Britis' race alright, my word!"
died when one of them mugged him for twenty quid.

The Policy continued to non-exist
for 80 years of white tea with sugar.

# Coningham v Coningham

As the colonies were uniting,
Arthur was divorcing Alice.
The co-respondent had been recommended
to Cardinal Moran by the Pope himself:
Father O'Haran. Fiercely prot.,
Arthur only wanted custody
of Alice's elder two, plus cash
for damages. The third he said was fathered
when she was Fathered. The revolver
he fired in the court when he lost the case
had been loaned to him by William Dill Macky,
the Presbyterian Gunman.

But Moran missed out on precedence
over the C of E on New Century's,
New Nation's Day thanks to the scandal.
The gunman, too, was miffed that his lot
weren't up there with Archbishop Smith and co.
So there weren't any Micks or Jocks at the do
and for weeks the sermons were thunderbolts
splitting the cobbled country into more than states.

# Black Cat and Wooden Shoe

Joe Hill "wouldn't be found dead in the state of Utah"
so his ashes went to Wobblies round the world.
Australia's portion was seized in a raid
before it could be decently interred
in the Botanical Gardens, ended up
in the fireplace of Central Police Station, Sydney,
not keeping the coppers nearly hot enough
so they warmed up by running through the streets
scraping off walls Tom Barker's poster,
the one urging bosses, parsons, editors
and landlords to war and workers to follow them.

It got hotter still when Tom was jailed.
Simpson's Bond Store, Stedman's, Winn's
all burned as beacons of war-bond investment,
Bryant and May the opposition spokesmen
for liberty. Better fire than blood,
or let the politicians cut their own throats
to dowse the flaming struggle.

# Waldheim

Purged from the Ulverstone Club lest it be seen
as fostering "a continent of Germans
and mongrels, or of yellow races",
Gustav trekked up to Cradle
six months after sweet Kate's death
to their forest home, their hideaway,
with memories of peace and tenderness.

The stove he lugged in was "heavy machinery",
the clothes line "a wireless aerial".
Why else would an enemy alien
want to command the high ground
except to spy, to sabotage, to cook up ways
of killing the nephews of the gentlemen
of the Ulverstone Club over in Flanders?

The Siegfried Line stretched to Daisy Dell, Dove Lake,
to keep the currawongs and ring-tails in Prussian discipline
and make the mountain ash grow Junker-straight?
While farmhands died twisted in Somme mud
the cockies here were all up-front for Hughes
and Empire Loyalty, but thankful for the secret ballot
to vote against conscripting the next crop's harvesters.

So Gustav stayed on the mountain, knew
the wildflowers' true subversion and the snow,
yelled in whatever Austrian dialect he needed
around the summits, into the storms.
His hermit's sanity under gross hewn beams
was a star way above the cultivated valleys
until the world could climb to meet him.

# The *Emden*

First they'd said the Russians had sunk her
somewhere off China. Down for six weeks,
she'd resurfaced in the Bay of Bengal.

Damned Huns never play fair. She sank five
British merchant ships, took their crews on board,
looked after them, made sure they got to safety.

This was still a courteous war. When we heard
that this time for certain she'd been captured,
surrendering after a single shot

from a British cruiser, we were reassured.
The game still had rules. God was umpiring
and even German batsmen walked.

That, too, proving false was too much to take.
Finally, off Cocos, the *Sydney* ran her down.
Although the *Ibuki* was faster and better armed

our oriental allies bowed to a need
more imperative than naval tactics,
let us teach them a lesson about games like war.

As Newbolt said, the boys on the *Sydney*
had all the musical abilities
of large marsupials. They knew, too,

how to sink the hind claw when the opponent's
down again and again and again long after
the fight's over. "Their hearts were hot."

Six months later Gallipoli
would make us great losers, but this established
the national image as nasty winners.


>Note: Sir Henry Newbolt's poem based on this incident contains the lines (referring to the sailors of the *Sydney*), "Their hearts were hot / and as they shot / they sang like kangaroos."

# Diggers

When Scullin's four bob at the siding
faded in the Mallee sun like everything
except the ink on the mortgage
it only took a phone call from Melbourne
and we were ready. If this was Gallipoli
again we were the Turks. The tykes,
reds and sussos could storm but never take
the heights of our decent pride. We dug
a trench across the highway at Ouyen,
manned it all night. They knew better than to try.

# Lockout

Next-door were lucky; they had cookery books,
read recipes around the table when they were hungry.
We didn't even have that. It was scab or starve.
John Brown had said, "Let them eat grass."
We held out. Dad was solid. Mum was a bunch of twigs.

Most of them were returned men, too, the ones
that were fired on at Rothbury, but some were kids,
or older, too slow or too naive to be safe,
like the old bloke who looked like he was tied
to the roadside gravel by a skein of blood

from his stomach, trying to push himself up,
or the young feller with two bullets lodged
in the loose skin under his jaw. But he survived,
which is more than our Norm did
after the dum-dum got him in the guts.

Cessnock lost 25 cricket teams thanks to
the lockout. Men who'd come through
Gallipoli, Salonika, the Dublin Post Office
or jail as COs only to be shot by Aussies found
if they won't let you work, you can't afford to play.

You know a town is really desperate
when the evangelists come to scavenge.
They filled one of the pits with water,
turned it into a great baptismal bath
to save whole families for John Brown's Jesus.

# Many Happy Returns: 26/1/1938

A carriage-load of Kooris was brought in
from the reserve at Menindee.
They were taken straight from the train and locked
in the Redfern police barracks stable,
guarded by dogs until the 26th.

Then they emerged, ready to play their part.
Wearing leaves, they were chased along the beach
by people dressed as British soldiers,
carrying bayonets. The organisers, it seemed,
hadn't needed to bring these people in specially
nor lock and guard them like a surprise gift.

Amateur historical and theatrical
society members just love
that sort of thing. Party games and dressing up
are marks of a civilised culture:
playhouse or drawing room, parliament or church.

After sharing a float in the parade
like jolly good fellows, the Kooris were sent back
next day to their tin sheds by the Darling.

# The Mayor

*after Frank Hardy*

When his missus had shot through
just before the Duke of Gloucester's visit
he needed a Lady Mayoress for the reception,
so hired a prostitute. She passed OK except
when she hitched up her skirt
and had a snake's in the hand basin.
After all, the Duke wouldn't have known
one working class colonial from another
and the Duchess kept her gloves on,
didn't need to wash her hands.

Then there was the time he drove
the Council's steamroller into the Yarra,
got a three hundred quid commission
on the sale of a new one. Fair enough
for a chuckle over a few gins years later.
He even steamrolled Wren's machine
and Keon's and the left to make
a building site for independence
in the inner suburbs. Local government
today is corporate, slick as soapy water,
plays Pilate to the old rorts.

But what the municipal incinerator burned
besides the waste from backyard abortions
and pre-selection ballot boxes
from unreliable wards, we'll never know.
"*Non corpus delicti*" Squizzy used to say—
"No corpse, no bloody inquest".
What do we wash our hands in when
we avoid judgement or before
we clap them or slap our thighs
for the larrikin battler and his heirs?
Are we sure it's sweeter than a whore's piss?

# Tanah Merah

A pencilled note thrown
to the wharf at Bowen from the *Both* was
a gap of white in the green curtain,
a peep-hole in hell's back door,
a scribbled PS to 20 years
of a future nation's leaders isolated
in "a specially appointed place"
malarial, rotting, ringed by ravines,
escape-proof. Thousands had been sent,
intellectuals, unionists, whole families.
Hundreds survived.

Was it chance their first landfall was Paterson's town?
Even miles up the Digul a wharfie knows where his mates are,
knows that despite the pink skin, big noses, foreign smell,
the angle of the bent backs is the same,
that not all blonds are bastards.
They would soon find out that in this country
not all bastards are bastards,
but those that are are real bastards.

When Mynheer Dr Van Der Plas
came up the Digul to address
his "fellow-countrymen"
and ship them to Australia,
he said he liked the Indonesian people.
So did the cannibals in the jungle around the camp.
The old and the sick were left.
Their deaths would not help the Japanese.
Australia had always been a safe place
to put superfluous humanity. It had been
a century since the last load.

# Red Nest in Vital Mine

*Sydney Sun 17/9/54*

When they've got you the sack
and you're sick of being burgled
by ASIO
you just piss off,
buy a farm on King Island
—far enough away
from Moscow, Berlin, Canberra—
and get some peace.

Fred Rose thought that,
but he forgot
about scheelite. Scheelite?
What the hell's that?
It's used to harden steel
and there's one big mine
in the free world. Free world?
That's a bit of a joke.

They'd had Fred lined up
to cop some shit
since '52
but nothing would stick.
So they followed him down
to his island farm
and they asked him to lie
at the Petrov Commission.

Fred could do with a loan
and he and Mr Menzies
would both like to get
a good night's sleep.
When they brought Fred back
to Canberra
he talked all right
but he talked about peace.

He talked about justice,
democracy.
That wasn't what
they wanted to hear,
so they asked about scheelite.
That one big mine
is on King Island
—just Fred's luck!

Of course there weren't any spies
and the scheelite mine's
now as dead as Ming.
But courage and truth
are still around
'cause now and then
a Fred Rose somewhere
takes a stand.

# Lake Eyre Curse

The locals call it Katitanda, won't walk on it.
Campbell came with his St Christopher and teddy bears
to prove that short-haired Tory con-men ruled OK
even in swinging '63, that superstition
would take a back seat to discipline every time,
and there were no back seats in the *Bluebird*; Mr Whoppit
(his favourite teddy) shared the cockpit. Discipline
and family tradition would bring the Empire back
from "pop and pleasure". Sir Malcolm (contacted
per medium) had given the parental thumbs-up.

It never rains, of course. That's the attraction, that and
the long hard flat of crust laid over clay and the lack
of green, his unlucky colour. Military
precision will prevail, make nonsense of the niggers'
irrational fears. It rained. Common sense and money
called it off for a year. It rained again. What the hell!
He went for it anyway, even on a Friday.
Between the two runs he saw his father in the windscreen
talking of fire and death in Utah. He broke the record.
Katitanda keeps its curse for things that matter.

# Advent: 21 Dec. 1967

In St Paul's the play
re-enacted and rehearsed a birth
while through and around the faithful audience
ASIO's backstage crew prepared
for the coming of LBJ
and his retinue of shepherds and crooks:
Thieu, Park, Marcos, Kittikachorn,
whose lambs had been stuck and left to spurt
all over South-East Asia
till the undertow of blood was stronger than Cheviot,
sucked and ripped more life more fiercely.

The wise men, by the way, stayed away,
responding to the appeal
by Police Commissioner Arnold:
"No demos by request".

This was the fifth day. The surf
had trundled nothing up, rolled no rocks aside.
Sea lice can inside twenty-four hours
stuff themselves with every morsel
of what makes the difference
between a PM and a skeleton.
By now they would be working on
the ligaments. By Tet there will be
unconnected bones.

You can't shoot sea lice with a speargun,
or bomb the tide away.

# Sight Screen

When Kim Hughes's tears
hardened to cataracts
only the gleam of rands
provided enough light to take guard
as the umpire gave him two legs.
He never got his eye in again.

Two legs are not enough to avoid
being run out by dogs and mace.
Blindness is only a virtue in justice,
or else black and white look unalike
and a keen eye can pick out
a lethal delivery against a coloured crowd.

And now the laager louts are in,
cutting and glancing to the darkest boundaries
of sponsors' visions, piling on the runs:
another Great Southern Stand to cheer.
What is the sawdust soaking up
on the run-up to freedom?

The slow-mo replay keeps repeating
scenes where the red on clothes
doesn't come from polishing the ball.
No matter how advanced
the electronic scoreboard is
there are some sundries it can't record.

# Footscray FC

*for and after Martin Flanagan*

Down the street from the Bulldog Florist
the community mural shows John Shaw Neilson
and Dougie Hawkins. It was made too early
for scenes from *Romper Stomper* or to portray
Irene Chatfield, the scraggers' saviour.

When they fought the merger in '89
there was even one bloke with a German accent
wearing lederhosen and a St Kilda jumper
who doorknocked North Altona and collected
bags of silver coins to help keep the 'Dogs.

Back in '33, the chain strike at Angliss's,
there were no local scabs; they had to bring them in
from the country. Later, one of them
was recruited by the Bulldogs.
The rest of the team wouldn't even train with him.

# The Streets Aren't For Dreamers

# The Cull

Don't they know it's going on already?
Where do they live? Where do their kids live?
São Paulo, Flinders Street Station, Dagenham:
you don't need to stay at school to learn that kind
of geography. Same planet, same street.
My koori mate Shane's got a brother in Robinvale.
You don't know what happens there? Get real!

Cops and Wormald guards are just the tip,
methodical, uniformed, doing their job.
The real bulk's deeper, where the ice-white shirts
of management trainees are medalled
only with pen clips over the heart
from nine to five, but after dark …

How much shit does it take to fill
a four-wheel drive? How much
self-righteousness need squeeze into one
trigger finger? Do they think
beef-faced Old Grammarians can play
football forever, not want new sport?

The light at the end of the tunnel
is mounted on roo bars and it burns
like a tyre necklace or a church barbecue.

"It couldn't happen here," say the newspapers
inside my shirt and pants against the wind
round the back of the Frosto plant.

A Landcruiser's headlights switch the mesh fence on.

# Rat's Song

This is a great town.
We got the Post Office steps
where we hang out
and sometimes talk about things.
We got the car park
where you can score what you need.
It could be better ...

      if it weren't for the board room voodoo charts
      and the flash-tied bum-boys vomiting "Sell!"
      into carphones, if it weren't for the smiles
      of greased and grateful consultants when
      a nod on the shuttle flight's as good as a drink
      at the island bar in the chairman's pool;
      if it weren't for the heaven of merchant banks
      where the Zegna'd angels bray their praise
      from the BRW hymnal, then
      this town might seem a bit less like hell;

... if we had Timezone
and indoor cricket and jobs.
But it's a great town.
The cops don't hassle you much.
We got a milk bar
with a jukebox and all.

# Stage Dive

Not always living by proxy, nor reliving
the clip of edited glamour thrash,
the fantasy death gig safe as the States,
no, sometimes, having so heavy a need to fly
on a lead break of my own, to assert
more than dreary frenzy can: noise pure beyond sound,
a tattoo sharper than art or pain,
I make and am still and private.

Anyone can jump from the top of an amp
into a crowd. Faith in the music, in the stance,
is a bungy rope. You might as well
sit in the mall or round a bong.
You might as well muttter, "The world's fucked"
to your mates who know that's not news.

"Despair" is no more to the point
than "the devil". When the metal
gets to be more than metaphor
it's style driven all the way
till it fuses with reality.

Like when Jason's head banged back
that night we were just having a few beers
no smart-arse video director
put the clotted pink crap
on my Anthrax T-shirt.

Now I mime to the tape of his suicide
but with feeling; the memory of his sudden weight
in my arms is the bass line to a track
I'll cut one day. When I dive
it will be through all this shit and on forever.

# Roadkill

The paws for jewellery, the skins
not big enough for clothes without a lot
of sewing, but good
for market kitsch.

Don't knock technology's overkill;
it hunts as byproduct. We gather,
living off and on the road,
subsistence driving.

Just as the birds have a caste system
so we clean carrion, denying ants
all but smears in the sun
red as our hands.

Your world needs our enterprise
as much as we need your crass diesel speed.
There are untouchable
hordes of us.

# Advice

Always look at their eyes. It weakens them
and brings slow thoughts they can't afford.
You get to know the best marks from eyes,
to avoid the mad, the scared, the smart.
Eyes hard as money are good for a challenge;
just don't expect to win every time.
Those softened by grog, TV or work
or flashing with outreach charity are best
for a touch, a con, an easy ride.

Diversify. If you get too hooked
on one line you'll end up being pinched.
Giving head to gents in Princes Square,
the five-finger discount at the bottle shop,
dealing, of course, running a couple of sorts:
there's plenty of games to win at; just don't get
too big for your Docs. And know your place.

The suburbs in daylight are a waste. Cruise there
for odd jobs or a raffle scam or casing
and they hit the phone. The white Commodore
snaps into the crescent like a pet to heel.
People who live in houses must be sick.
They say bricks and electricity give you cancer,
but it's their minds are worse: Neighbourhood Whatchacallit,
paranoia, there's enough of that in squats.
Don't mess with the kind that prunes and sweeps.

Above all, be always on the move
but always, at the centre, still.

# Words for K

So now he rapes my brain by saying "sorry"
and I bury my hair in cold sand,
swim naked in the winter ocean,
climb high to hell's ice.

Sixteen years of Daddy
bursting through clouds of brimstone dust
from the family bible, the chapel organ pumping
at my blood, at my baby innards, Mum's eyes
like vicious prayers, the circle closed
as a country congregation.

I was seventeen
when I first dared look in a mirror.
I still sleep on my stomach
in case Satan through the floorboard cracks
takes me by surprise again
to make me his favourite daughter.

And folders, drawers, rooms, mountains
won't hold all my words, my formulae,
my poems. There's no climate
the sane and faithful live in
that my statistics can describe.

Hold me but don't touch me.

# The Ballad of Tamieka Sharp, aged 15

Had a flat for a while with Kylie and Todd.
It was working out just fine.
We'd sit down each night with a joint or two
and a bottle of green ginger wine.

But there's better things than rent to spend money on
and the telly they sold was mine
so I split from there with a tape or two
and a bottle of green ginger wine.

Now Todd's moved in to his girlfriend's house
and Kylie's shacked up with Brian.
I'd be lonely except for a bloke or two
and a bottle of green ginger wine.

I ain't going near the welfare mob.
They treat you like shit, the swine.
I'll survive, you bet, with a trick or two
and a bottle of green ginger wine.

Went down to the Housing the other day,
stood for three hours in line.
They could get me a place in a year or two.
I didn't bother to sign.

But it's not too cold in a cave up the Gorge
where the moon makes the river shine,
in my thick black tights with a smoke or two
and a bottle of green ginger wine.

# Saturday Night

Next thing I know I'm on the gravel
of a car yard.
"Name and address?" There's a big old cop
like a cliff and the words would climb
but my lip's too thick to let them out
and the neon's slow pulse goes
    BRIGHT
"What's your name, son?"
    BLACK
    BRIGHT
There were
    BLACK
        three
    BRIGHT
"Where do you live?"
    BLACK
        of them
    BRIGHT
    BLACK
and they went
    TOO BRIGHT
        that way
but my arm won't point
    TOO BLACK
and is that rain or blood or piss? Don't care.

And then he's gone.
Somewhere across the street
someone's playing Cold Chisel's "Saturday Night".
Now the light's trampolining on the duco again
and if I lie here a bit longer I'll be right
to walk home. My legs don't hurt.
The music helps.

# Bouncer

You're here for fun? Have fun.
You're here for trouble? I'm a wall.

In there is a wall of sound, built
by the crazy masons of Spector's guild.
Between us it's safe as a hilltop city.
Mirror balls fill your drinks with gew-gaws.
Colour and commerce flash. Sweat dances
across the rainbow, zydeco to house.

I face the street, a black plain
random with calls, tracer tail-lights,
knots of pain, cold marauders.

Past my trim gut the believers
in their best market gear
file in like villagers.

# Escort

Bucking with fake joy I syphon
your pride and let it soften
in the lather of our bargain.
You were the hard man, the men,
all my uncles, landlord
of every clammy flat. Now
I'm getting the rent easy
as moaning. More slippery
than any fancy drink and with
a twist, I've knocked you out
for all your jabbing. Sport
you would call it, but what's
in my purse is the price
of admission. Blind spectator,
you had thought you were winning.
Smile your limp thanks and dream
of another tough day.
When I walk to the cab rank
clad in my skirt my stiletto
heels will be rigid but the night
will ooze, fluid, around me.

# Busking

Outside Myer, outside the bank,
trying to crack the silence of cold wind,

give 'em Diamond, give 'em MOR.
No-one can think and shop at the same time.

Three days a week makes food and dope
and a place to write the songs they'll never hear

about them, what they did to old Liam
with his uke and squeezebox down the Mall:

fifties folk hero, contracts, fans, all the best clubs,
now the booze and I are out to beat him.

Or what they do to each other: "The Ballad of
the Great Sale Day Disaster", "Ode to

the Plain Clothes Cop". I could give 'em
enough social comment to fill a car park.

And love songs, too, not this cute slop
but riffs and words torn from the live guts,

that flay the throat in passing, tunes as chunks
of fire and flames of skin to drench the air

with sex and pain, make them feel their need
to die now or live as flesh forever.

You can't be a star unless you are a sun
of stinking gases, uninhabitable.

I'll make it. Meanwhile, the last toddler's
been dragged from the toyshop to the car seat.

Time to pack up. As I go past old Liam
I'll drop a couple of bucks in his uke case.

# The Hoon's Soliloquy

Friday night and the last brawl
outside the Royal's ended.
The last two cops stalk through the Mall.
Not much to do in town at all
except, perhaps, to gutter crawl
and that's not recommended.

A blockie or two, then for a thrill
let her snarl as the fatties spin.
Fishtail up the George Street hill,
lay down rubber on asphalt till
the streets are paved with it. Drive to kill.
Live to drive and to win.

There's a slab in the back for later on;
out Youngtown way there's a barbie.
Should be a chick there I can con,
some schoolgirl bimbo simpleton.
A drink and a chat then we'll be gone.
Tomorrow I'll work on the carbie.

# Arriving in Devonport

Driving into a smashed-bottle sunset,
tape-deck spilling k d like blood and honey
into a pit, I know just how the next town waits.

Oil tanks patrol the river bank where the bridge reaches,
tentative, into the back-lit heart, a syringe of hope.
I'm sliding with the music through the streets.

I know the pubs will smell of guns, divorce,
dealerships and bigotry: too flat, too shallow
for any despair deeper than talk-back summons.

No matter how smartly plate-glass fashion slices
the hum of truth from the drum of lust for distance
hope doesn't empty showrooms or fill freezer-packs.

This town knows that. I park, cut the music
with the motor. In the river local wisdom slaps
the hull of the ferry to the anxious world.

# Blue Cow at the Trades

The heat sticks wet smoke to the back of my neck
and I'll ignore them ignoring me
those cool art students.
I only came for the lyrics
but the mixer's got it wrong so I'll
bob on the shoreline between dancers and drinkers,
a generation's flotsam having a night out
with my beer parked safely
and afterwards drive home
under the limit, alone.

When I was their age
and you could hear the words
things were much as they are now
not cool enough, too cool perhaps,
I'd peck at items like a wading bird
ready to dart to or from
the sea's electric music but not to fly
except on the long haul between homes.
Some lives have big patterns not discernible
to those who are always on their own hot beach.

# The Leaving

Adventure! Only rich kids went on camps
or loonies in long socks from the South
singing daft songs on the moors.

This was better. This was a big ship
and a bright land, a quarry for hacking
the future into chunks of light.

They sliced me from greasy sleet,
from sticky alleys of games and,
on some cleaner wharf, from my sister.

Then sweat and shredded fingers under
a sky that whipped us: the only soothing
from each other's rough hands, chapped lips.

Since then, the seasonal plod,
odd job to door to odd glimpse
of what might. Funny to hear

those flashes of Mersey Sound
from trannies in huts, between
races in country pubs. Not that I ...

Now, too torn and slow to pick,
even to drift, I'm sat here
in another grey city's cold rain.

# Bear

When they put that play on
down at the community centre
I was a bear. I scared the first three rows
of welfare workers silly.

Mostly when I roar it's not an act,
more of a drama. The worst thing
is not being able to tell them,
clearly, to shut up.

Not drunk, not stupid, only
angry: I won't get in that bus
with SPASTIC painted on it;
I am grizzly with pride,

polar with disdain. In the street
I lumber, shamble, but in
the straight line of the hunt.
I am not cuddly.

# Chrome, Bone & Microphone

Light Verse / Performance Pieces
1984–2003

# Life

You might say I'm a drifter, an aimless sort of bloke
whose most profound pronouncement is a weakish little joke.
When controversy rages and arguments are rife
I'll be floating just like algae in the swimming pool of life.

I tried hard not to worry. I tried hard not to mind
when my house burned down, my dog was shot and my little boy
                                                    went blind,
but since my boss has sacked me and run off with my wife
I'm lying like an oil stain on the garage floor of life.

But you must look on the sunny side. It's no use feeling blue.
We all have trials to face to see if we'll come smiling through.
So I'll be bright and I'll be tough, no matter what the strife,
like a little plastic spaceman in the Corn Flakes box of life.

# Life Education for Rural Youth

Well I started out on Tiguvon, but soon hit the harder stuff.
I was knocking back the Warbex just to prove I was cool and tough.

Avomec? 'Ave a 'andful! and wash 'em down with Riporon.
Just a coupla shots of Telmin and a dose or three of Alfacron.

When I need a little something to help me make it through the night
I just phone up the man from Websters and get a fix of Rumevite.

When the ragwort's taken over and the dams have all run dry,
sell a truckload of vealers and buy a few months supply

of Permaco or Closal and you will soon forget
how ruinous the times are. How about some Agronet?

If your accountant's gone to Risdon and your kids are voting green,
a dash of Nilverm in your coffee will help you stay serene.

You could go and shoot your neighbour, whip a serf or two or
                                               swear at your horse,
but you're better off with Vaxall—let the chemistry run its sweet
                                                           course.

You'll be higher than the price of superfine with Systemex.
You could sneer at Rod O'Connor when you're full of Fasinex.

Try Pegasol or Nucidol. We all need some sort of crutch.
Glyphosate will bring you down again. Just don't do too much

till you know what you can handle. My old uncle nearly died
from a bum trip on Vanellus, and it's worse with Duracide.

You city slickers think you've got it made with angel dust
and coke and crack and ecstasy—until you cop a bust.

But they can't stick you for possession of a block of Ultrapro.
At the Campbell Town show the other week I was feeling kinda low,

so I dropped a coupla items from the Nufarm catalogue.
I won three sheepdog trials—and I hadn't brought me dog!

There's a lot of great traditions in this wide and sunburnt land,
like poisoning the waterholes, like holding out your hand

for gov'ment subsidies, like wearing Drizabones and driving Mercs
and union bashing, but there's more to it than whingeing, droughts
                                                                and perks,

and if you read the tales of the great outback then surely you will
                                                                                     know
that Henry Lawson's dog was loaded, and Clancy of the Overflow

saw visions splendid. What was he on? Prob'ly Tedox is my guess,
cut with LI 700. Bet his frontal lobes were a mess.

So if you see a poor old cocky looking strung out and in pain,
just pump him full of Valbazen and he'll be right as rain.

# Time

There are times when time doesn't need a face,
when your pulse is enough if you're smart,
when her eyes are a liquid crystal display
just as clear as the quartz in her heart
and the pendulum that's swung one too many times
has made its final swing for sure.
The little hand's pointing to the top of the clock
but the big hand's pointing out the door.

What's the time, Mr Wolf? It's a quarter past hell
and dinner time's not on the menu.
It's that time of night, of the month, of the year;
it's the time of your life but when you
clock up the hours that add up to a life
you know that the answer's a lie.
The little hand's stubbing out a cigarette
and the big hand's waving goodbye.

# Road

Well I've left some of myself on every motel sheet from here to
                                                            Surfers,
dying just a little bit each time I hit the road,
'cause it's lonely out there and the world is full of strangers
but it's worse if you're stuck somewhere where there's nowhere else
                                                            to go.

So it's plane or train or thumb and it's make it to the next gig,
read another bunch of poems in another hazy pub.
And all the lonely people who are dying to be writers
or just come along to listen to another lonely man

they just clap or laugh politely, then go home when the show's over
leaving me with just the barman and a pile of unsold books.
But the cheque is in the mail and I'll buy another bottle
and tomorrow is another day, another airport lounge.

I've stashed my pride for safety in a railway station locker.
When you do the wandering minstrel bit you've got to travel light
'cause the road is long and rocky and it's just as full of clichés
as a country and western song and you must leave room for hope.

# Katoomba Tourist Poem

Well, I've seen the Three Sisters, that's Yoko,
Hanako and Kimiko, all their cousins
and the rest of the coach-tour crew.
I called your name at Echo Point
and got your answering machine.
I bought a set of souvenir place-mats;
they all had pictures of you,
so I stood for a while at the edge of the cliff.
And they reckon the mountains are blue.

I learned all about geology
and avifauna, too,
learned that Ranger MacKay cut all those steps
and that Aaron Rainer is a cocksucking bastard
according to the graffiti at Honeymoon Point
where I didn't jump, but made the mistake
of concentrating on the view,
so I slipped on a condom. That is to say,
I slipped
(on a condom)—there were quite a few.
But I never found Divorce Lookout.
And they reckon the mountains are blue.

# Encounter: A True Story

Through the misty jungles where no-one interferes
the Liawep had wandered for 50,000 years

until by chance they stumbled, in 1993,
across a public servant who offered them some tea.

Their noble isolation meant they didn't know this brew.
The kindly public servant then asked, "One lump or two?"

Now sugar was another thing they hadn't met before.
Ah! Civilisation! But there was even more.

In the town of Telefomin, a few days' trek away
the Baptists had a mission where they taught folk how to pray.

When they heard about the Liawep they sang loud hymns of praise.
Here was a chance to win some souls from brutish, pagan ways.

The Telefomin Baptists then set out on a search
to find the heathen Liawep and build for them a church.

The Liawep are nomads, tend neither field nor flock.
They carry their god with them in the shape of a small rock.

So somewhere in the jungle stands a lonely sentinel,
the Liawep First Baptist Church, an empty, useless shell.

While in another clearing of the Liawep's green world
they sip lapsang from china cups with little fingers curled.

The moral of this story is, if you don't stay still,
the Baptists mightn't track you down but the public service will.

# Lime-green Widgie

Twelve or thirteen,
used to go foxin'.
I was the youngest:
kept cockatoo.
Down Fern Glade or
up by the waterfall,
never caught anyone
—somethin' to do.
I was always stalkin'
my lime-green widgie,
singin' Buddy Holly songs
and wearin' Mitchell blue.

Friday night shopping,
up and down Wilson Street,
never bought anythin'
just hangin' roun'.
Wish I looked like Elvis.
Wish I played the guitar.
Wanna do somethin'
to shake this town.
My lime-green widgie,
teased hair and tight skirt,
cardigan buttoned up
wrong way round.

Sittin' in the Bluebird,
milkshakes and jukebox,
standin' roun' the doorway
at the surf club dance,
wore all the right clothes,
denim and pink socks.
Never had a Harley.
Never had a chance.

My lime-green widgie
worked at the pulp mill,
dated blokes with genuine
grease on their pants.

So there went yesterday
wobblin' on her high heels
into tomorrow,
leavin' me blue
and I'm still stalkin'
my lime-green widgie,
singin' Jimmy Clanton songs.
And I'm 62.

# Too Old To Rap

I could rap about the times
we live in with rhymes
that come easy and sweet
with a simple beat,
could say "No oil spills.
No dams. No mills."
It's easy being green
if it doesn't mean
much more than a chant
and a smug little rant
in front of the mike
'cause none of us like
nuclear waste
or the lack of taste
in tomatoes these days,
ultraviolet rays
burning up our skin.
And we know it's a sin
to destroy and pollute.
But it's just too cute:
I perform and you clap.
I'm still young enough
to strut my stuff
but I'm too old to rap.

I could rap for a while
about rhythm and style.
I grew up with be-bop
but this new hip-hop
with its fast line of patter
is a different matter.
I can hack the pace
but there's not much grace
in the two-stress line.

Perhaps it's a sign
of middle age,
though I still like to rage.
I go back past the frug
to the jitterbug,
but I'll have a bash
at heavy metal thrash
and I'll nod when you say
that punk's passé.
When I'm out on the town
I don't fall down
the generation gap.
I'm not too old
to rock 'n' roll
but I'm too old to rap.

# The Ballad of Dennis Archer

He had an alsatian named Misty,
the best dog for miles around,
but Misty one day bit a neighbour
so there was talk of putting her down.
He loved that dog
more than life itself.

So Dennis went into depression,
Dennis went into despair,
'cause life for him without Misty
would be more than he could bear.
He loved that dog
more than life itself.

Now Dennis had a wife who loved him.
He didn't want her to grieve
so he chopped her up with a hatchet
before he took his leave.
He loved that dog
more than life itself.

Then he climbed up to the rooftop
and he took a mighty leap.
He landed on the driveway
in a bloody, broken heap.
He loved that dog
more than life itself.

But, all unknown to Dennis,
the neighbour wasn't going to sue.
His wife had asked her to drop the case
because, of course, she knew
he loved that dog
more than life itself.

# All I've Planned and All I've Schemed

Alf O'Meagher rides, not again,
but for the first time this time
in a crimson Giulietta, the kids in the back,
hitting it out of the sun to the coast.

He's wearing a black denim jacket
with the sleeves torn off and listening
to a tape of the soundtrack of the remake
of *Breathless*; he pretends that he's thinking

he's Richard Gere playing the part
of Jesse Lujack alias Jack Burns, who thinks
he's Jerry Lee Lewis, who is.
He knows he's not really thinking that.

Somewhere between the third playground
and the second vomit-stop he changes the cassette
to Jivin' Jim Barnes taped from 2SER FM
in '83. Nostalgia shows ain't what they used to be.

But he doesn't change his jacket. The Alfa slows
past the incongruous moderne butchers' shops
and the cafes bright with Port Arthur tea-towels.
He only passes when it's safe, thinking of the end.

Picking up objects of art in his headlights
and wondering, "Am I real or only
human?" and "Did I invent Jimmy Clanton
singing 'Just a Drea-eam' or was that really human?"

he moves into an epiphany of false honour
beyond time and light, metal and sound.
The process of arriving disturbs his banality.
Oh, how he longs for the complex life!

## Aubade

I'm waiting till the kettle boils or Godot comes, or spring.
I light another cigarette and scratch a bit and yawn,
my elbows on the laminex, my head in no-man's-land.
There's empty stubbies on the floor and a fire truck on the lawn.

Out of deference to decency I won't describe my tongue.
I'd check to see what's in the fridge but the light'd hurt my eyes.
I wish I could remember what I said to those two cops.
I think I quoted Swinburne, which may not have been wise.

But at least they went away again, which is more than I can say
for the fourteen angry skinheads, three nuns and the crocodile.
God knows who or what I slept with. I didn't dare to look.
But if a thing's worth doing it's worth doing it with style.

*112*

# The Nature of Australia

Nature's OK, I s'pose, but it's too big
and "small is beautiful"'s what I've been taught.
"Waste not." Why then so many leaves and birds?
The distances between cities should be short.

Look at Belgium. They don't need scenery.
They do all right. Or take, e.g., Hong Kong:
maximum efficient use of space.
Trouble with us, our packaging's all wrong.

We rattle round like Jaffas in a box
that's 90% air. The image lies.
We'd be had up for fraud if we were selling.
This country ought to be cut down to size.

> *Don't be so stupid. Think of our kids' kids*
> *and so on. They're all gonna need some space,*
> *their own trees to chop down and roos to shoot.*
> *Think of the future of the human race.*

# To Edmond's (*pace* Bill)

*Razzle dazzle*, little comet,
hurled like some celestial vomit
through the solar system, then
rock around the sun again.

*Burn that candle*, entertain us
disappearing up Uranus.
*Dim dim the lights*, go make a crater.
See ya later, Halleygator.

# Ten Minute Man ?

*On being asked to read ten minutes' worth of X-rated
poetry at the National Poetry Festival, Melbourne 1997*

I'm 53, I smoke too much, and drink.
The circulation's third-rate. The prostate's prostrate.
Ten minutes? When I was younger
I could have kept it up for longer,
given you an X-rated hour
and I would have begged for more.

Peter Cundall once observed
that when men reach middle age
they feel the need to chop down
all the tall trees in their gardens.
When I turned forty I invented the poetry cup.

At least I didn't call it a slam,
thank you ma'am.

# Midland Highway Blues

It's a long way to Heaven.
It's a long way to Hobart.
It's a long way to hitchhike
to either one.

And all those Volvos
with iridescent fish signs
on their rear windows
just cruise on by.

I'm an old fellow traveller,
dialectical materialist.
I don't believe in Hobart,
don't believe in Hell.

Don't believe in destinations
and I never trust signposts.
Never fell for that romantic
idea of the road.

But there's asphalt and semis,
white lines, gravel edges
and pilgrims in Volvos
who never stop.

But here I am in Hobart.
Must be some kind of miracle.
I hitched a ride with an atheist
who was heading somewhere else.

If you can drive a Volvo
through the eye of a needle
then you might get to Heaven,
but that's about all,

'cause if you're heading for Hobart,
no matter what you're driving,
the other end of the needle
is the one you'll need.

And the tripping pilgrims
who cross the Jordan
find the road winds downhill
to the very end.

But downhill or uphill,
Spring Hill or Constitution,
they all put their foot down
through St Peters Pass.

So if you ever see me
standing by the highway,
say, somewhere round Tunbridge,
sticking out my thumb,

then pay no attention
to which way I'm facing,
'cause if you're halfway to Heaven
all roads lead to home.

Just stick me in your back seat
and take me where you're heading.
I'm an old easy rider
who finds the going hard.

# Pension Payday

Today is pension payday and they're gathering at the Crown
and Jimmy's on the hustle and Maggie's on the town.
The bloke that runs the meat tray reckons everyone should pray
but the form guide in the paper says it's slow to dead today.

The day hit like paraldehyde, an undigested sun
was thrown up on the footpath and Bill's the only one
with guts enough to take it on. That's what I heard him say.
The form guide in the paper says it's slow to dead today.

The medication's being minded, lined along the kitchen bench.
There's a lot of scores to settle and a lot of thirst to quench.
There's some of us are shooting through and some of us will stay
and the form guide in the paper says it's slow to dead today.

Someone's broken off a bottle neck and something's free at last.
You'd hope that it's the future but it smells more like the past.
There's a kid with a new Sherrin but no-one wants to play
and the form guide in the paper says it's slow to dead today.

You can hardly hear the sirens for the sound of breaking glass.
Maggie's in the corner with her skirts up round her arse
and Jimmy's shat himself again and Bill's been put away
and the form guide in the paper says it's slow to dead today.

Someone somewhere said he wouldn't, then he thought he might.
There'll be bloodstains on the lino in the boarding house tonight
'cause today is pension payday and someone's gonna pay
and the form guide in the paper says it's slow to dead today.

# Why my Heart Belongs to Rover

You treated my heart like a frisbee.
It spun in a graceful arc.
You treated my heart like a frisbee.
You just wanted to play in the park.

You treated my heart like a frisbee.
You gave it a backhand flip.
You treated my heart like a frisbee,
tossed away our relationship.

You treated my heart like a frisbee.
It curved way overhead.
No-one thought it was worth catching,
so now the dog has it instead.

# At the Book Launch

"The author once said
it was his task
to put the sex back into poetry
and the poetry back into sex.
He has achieved this."

And from every woman in the crowded room
a spontaneous murmur:
"Bullshit."

Well, the book's fantastic
and you can't say
he didn't try.

## Ode to the Irenicists, c. 1987

You can rant in the halls
and paint on the walls
and march till your feet are sore,
vote NDP,
drink herbal tea
and think you're stopping war.

But it's Ron and Bob*
who'll do that job;
they're trying. They'll try harder
when they have faced
a little taste
of what they gave Grenada.

Back in the 'Nam
old Uncle Sam
came on pretty heavy, remember?
But the Viet Cong
made him look as strong
as Collingwood in September.

So don't turn the cheek,
'cause you know the meek
will only inherit ashes.
Let's cut the crap
and bomb Pine Gap;
and as for all the fascists ...

well, I've decided
they're just misguided,
they fell for some clever lies.
No need to hate 'em,
just re-educate 'em
right between the eyes.

*Former political leaders of the USA and one of its client states respectively.

# Writing with Viagra

She said she hoped I wouldn't be offended, but ...
I said, "Nothing ever offends me",
forgetting for the moment
war, poverty, racism, sexism, child abuse and the Liberal Party
—as you do—
"I've got a present for you," she said
and gave me a pen,
white, with a blue clip on which was stamped "Pfizer"
and strong red Vs like ticks all over it.
I use it to write soft, tender, limpid love poems.
Once I loaned it to another poet
and she snapped the clip off.
It had got loose and wobbly anyway.

I wasn't offended.

# Galilee Revisited

Another maudlin sunset,
another viscous drink:
it's too late to be randy
and it's far too soon to think.

Another lonely night of Sara Lee,
but even she keeps sliding off my knee.

Ask not for whom the Drum rolls,
which poet to invoke.
Wring out the wine-cask bladder
and light another smoke.

Another night of Cohen on CD.
Play it again, Len, play it again for me.

# Green and Blue: a love poem

When the ozone's shot to pieces and the war zone's spreading wide,
when the 'dozers and the priests have done their bit,
when the world's become a greenhouse and we're all Kentucky fried,
will you love me then? or still think I'm a shit?

When a handful of survivors wait on every mountain top,
just a few Jehovah's Witnesses, the AIDS virus and us,
all wondering when Dick Smith's chopper's gonna stop
and take us up to heaven like a bus,

when the final showdown's over and the Taliban has won,
will you look back on lost chances with regret?
When Rupert Murdoch's bought up all nine planets and the sun,
will you turn to me and sweetly say, "Not yet"?

# My Mate Robbo

My mate Robbo can always pick chicks up.
He's got this sure-fire technique.
He's not what you'd call handsome.
He's got a pathetic physique.
He's no great conversationalist.
He's not even all that well hung.
He sits alone in the singles bar,
just parting his hair—with his tongue.

# Salamanca Two Dog Blues

It's past midnight at Round Midnight and you still haven't showed.
One more bracket of Black Napkin for the road
then I'll stumble down and try to work out where I parked the car,
but first I'll get another Two Dog from the bar.

Downstairs the gig is over and the fans are home in bed.
You've been at some disco raging on instead.
So you didn't catch my reading, didn't join in the applause.
You missed my act and I sure am missing yours.

So I'm knocking back the Two Dogs and I'm listening to the band:
another night that didn't go as planned.
And maybe it's the saxophone or maybe it's the booze
makes it easier to put up with the blues.

All the other lonely drunks are getting grimly into pairs.
I should hide my Two Dog blues like they hide theirs,
save them for the coffee and the early morning news.
But that's real pain. I'd rather have the blues.

# Rimbaud: First Blood

He's on a mission and that's just where he belongs!
He's told not to derange the senses.
"Just write poems," they say.
But telling Rimbaud to hold back
is like ordering a rattlesnake not to bite.
RIMBAUD'S UNLEASHED AND NO-ONE'S GOING TO STOP HIM.
Rimbaud's dropped in to Paris to find out
if there are still any poets about.
There's one, Verlaine. They fall in love.

A drunken boat or a helicopter:
small, unfit, gay and French
or Stallone, wherever you spend
your season in Hell, there's a hero
to spend it with and illuminations
aren't always on a screen.

# Everything, 2002

Little Johnny Howard, every time he speaks,
has his tongue wedged firmly between George W's cheeks.
Stem cell research? Not on! I think that every embryo
should have the right to grow and grow and grow and grow and grow
until it has developed to be big enough at least
to accommodate the lust of Christian Brother and of priest.
Now smallpox comes in aerosol, so grab a can today.
In church, mosque, temple, synagogue, just holler, "Let us spray!"
To sum up all these world affairs—who's who and what is what—
is simple: There's Saddam Hussein and George W who's not.

# Haiku

High cue or low cue:
As long as they don't give me
a bent cue, I'll shoot.

High queue or low queue:
As long as I don't have to
stand in a long queue.

High Kew or low Kew:
Better than over the bridge
there in Collingwood.

High coo or low coo:
Whatever octave the doves
use I shall listen.

Hike, you! Don't like you.
Just piss off and stop writing
short Jap'nese poems.

# Cutting a Pretentious Tasmanian Poet Down to Size, or Effects of Light Verse

## 1. L'ton

Patchy town, lots of hills,
not much culture, light on thrills,
class divisions quite severe:
lucky the mad poet's here.
He can make a molotov
cocktail, and his philosoph-
y's quite simple: don't just wait
on your bum, perambulate.
Get to know your city well
before you blow it all to hell.

## 2. RIP Jen

You were a bit of a loner.
Most folk thought you were mad.
You hit the bottle down at your shack
and you died on your own. Too bad!
You'd really stuffed your liver,
but your nerve, to the end, was game.
They put you six feet under
and life went on much the same.

## 3. An adolescent considers his attitude towards an ordered society

He sits in the cafeteria
with tea and a cigarette.
His thoughts are getting drearier.
The table's getting wet.
He tries self-willed insanity;

perhaps they'll lock him away.
But, vanity, all is vanity,
and it's such a sunny day.